FIVE EPIC DISASTERS

ALSO BY LAUREN TARSHIS

I SURVIVED

THE SINKING OF THE *TITANIC*, 1912

THE SHARK ATTACKS OF 1916

HURRICANE KATRINA, 2005

THE BOMBING OF PEARL HARBOR, 1941

THE SAN FRANCISCO EARTHQUAKE, 1906

THE ATTACKS OF SEPTEMBER 11, 2001

THE BATTLE OF GETTYSBURG, 1863

THE JAPANESE TSUNAMI, 2011

THE NAZI INVASION, 1944

THE DESTRUCTION OF POMPEII, AD 79

FIVE EPIC DISASTERS

by Lauren Tarshis

SCHOLASTIC PRESS / NEW YORK

ISBN 978-0-545-78224-1

Text copyright © 2014 by Lauren Tarshis

All rights reserved. Published by Scholastic Press, an imprint of Scholastic Inc., *Publishers since 1920.* SCHOLASTIC, SCHOLASTIC PRESS, and associated logos are trademarks and/or registered trademarks of Scholastic Inc.

Library of Congress Cataloging-in-Publication data available.

12 11 10 9 8 7 6 5 4 3   15 16 17 18/0

Printed in the U.S.A.   23

First printing, October 2014

Designed by Deborah Dinger, Yaffa Jaskoll, and Jeannine Riske

To all of you amazing readers, who
make writing such a joy.

CONTENTS

AUTHOR'S NOTE

Dear Readers,

Over the past few years, I've received thousands of notes and e-mails from you, asking amazing questions — about writing, about research, about my family, and of course about my dog. But one of the most common questions has been: What was the inspiration for the I Survived series?

The answer is in this book.

When I'm not writing the I Survived books, I'm doing my job as editor of the Scholastic magazine *Storyworks,* which is read by more than 700,000 kids in their classrooms. The heart of every issue of *Storyworks* is a thrilling nonfiction article, and over the years I have written dozens and dozens of these articles myself. There are fascinating true stories about a huge range of subjects — incredible journeys and heroic people, death-defying rescues and real-life monsters, amazing inventions and shocking discoveries.

And, of course, I've written about disasters — tornadoes and shipwrecks and hurricanes and volcanoes and earthquakes and even a flood of molasses that filled the streets of Boston. I've written so many disaster stories for *Storyworks* that one friend nicknamed me "the disaster queen." I decided that was a compliment!

It was while writing these stories that I had the idea for the I Survived series. But it's not really the disasters themselves that captivate me. Sure, it's interesting to read about spewing lava and wild waves and winds whirling at 200 miles per hour. But what really fascinates me are the *people* in these stories — ordinary people who behave in heroic ways, who endure terrible events and go on to live happy lives. It's this human quality — *resilience* — that inspires me, and is at the heart of each of the I Survived books.

The stories you're about to read have appeared

in *Storyworks* in recent years, though I've expanded them for this collection and added new facts and interesting tidbits. Though the I Survived books are historical fiction, I think you'll see many similarities between those books and the nonfiction articles that follow.

Thank you all for making me a part of your reading journey!

Lauren Tarshis

#1

THE CHILDREN'S BLIZZARD, 1888

January 12, 1888, dawned bright and sunny in Groton, Dakota Territory, a tiny town on America's enormous wind-swept prairie. For the first time in weeks, eight-year-old Walter Allen didn't feel like he was going to freeze to death just by waking up. He kicked off his quilt and hopped out of bed with hardly a shiver. Within minutes he had thrown on his clothes, wolfed down his porridge, and kissed his mom good-bye. With a happy wave, he hurried off to school, a four-room schoolhouse about a half mile from his home.

All across Dakota Territory and Nebraska that morning, thousands of children like Walter headed to school with quicker steps than usual. For weeks they'd been trapped in their homes by dangerously cold weather. In some areas, the temperature had plunged to 40 degrees below zero. It was cold enough to freeze a person's eyes shut and turn their fingers blue and their toes to ice. Schools all through the region had been closed. Parents kept their kids inside, huddled close to stoves.

At least Walter's family lived in a proper house, on Main Street. His dad, W. C., was a lawyer and a successful businessman. But most of the people living on this northern stretch of prairie were brand-new settlers. They had come from Europe, mainly Sweden, Norway, and Germany. The majority were very poor and struggling to survive in this punishing land. Without money to buy a house or building supplies, thousands lived in bleak sod houses, tiny dwellings built from bricks of hardened soil. Life in a cramped, smoky "soddy" was never easy. Being trapped inside for weeks was torture.

What a relief it was to be back at school! It was still cold outside, only about 20 degrees. But after the weeks of frozen weather, the air felt almost springlike. Many kids left home without their warm wool coats and sturdy boots. Walter wore just his trousers and woolen shirt. Girls wore their cotton dresses and leather shoes, their braids swinging merrily from their hatless heads. As children arrived at Walter's school, some stood outside on the steps. They admired the unusual color of the sky — golden, with just a thin veil of clouds. "Like a fairy tale," one of them said.

AN ARCTIC BLAST

But not everyone was smiling at the surprisingly warm weather and the glowing sky. Some people had learned the hard way that they should never trust the weather on America's northern prairie, especially in the winter. Wasn't there something spooky about the color of the sky? Wasn't it odd that the temperature had jumped more than forty degrees overnight? A Dakota farmer named John Buchmillar thought so. He told his twelve-year-old daughter, Josephine, that she'd be staying put that day. "There's something in the air," he said to her with a worried glance at the sky.

There was indeed something in the air, and it was headed directly toward America's vast midsection. High up in the sky, three separate weather systems — masses of air of different temperatures — were about to crash together. The warm air that had delighted the school-children that morning would soon smash into a sheet of freezing Arctic air speeding down from Canada. Most dangerous of all was a low-pressure system — a spinning mess of unstable air churning its way across the continent from the northeast. The meeting of these three weather systems would soon create a monstrous blizzard, a frozen white hurricane of terrifying violence.

But Walter Allen and his classmates had no idea what was brewing above them in the endless

In a true blizzard, so much snow fills the air
that it can be impossible to see.

prairie sky. Not even the experts knew what was coming. First Lieutenant Thomas Woodruff, trained in the brand-new science of weather forecasting, was working at his office in Saint Paul, Minnesota. It was Woodruff's job to gather information about the weather, including the temperature and wind speeds, in surrounding areas. Using this information, Woodruff would try to predict what weather was heading down to the area around Groton.

At 3:00 P.M. the day before, Woodruff had sent out his prediction for the following day. His forecast would be printed in small-town newspapers.

"For Minnesota and Dakota: Slightly warmer fair weather, light to fresh variable winds."

AN EXPLOSION

All morning Walter Allen sat at his desk working on his arithmetic problems. His teacher walked through the room offering help, her skirt swishing and her boots clicking against the wooden floor. The children worked on their small rectangular chalkboards, which were called writing slates. After finishing each set of problems, Walter took a tiny glass perfume bottle from his desk, removed the jewel-like lid, and poured a drop of water onto the hard surface of his slate. The bottle was Walter's prized possession.

All of the other children kept small bottles of water and rags at their desks to wipe their slates clean. But Walter's bottle was special, a treasure that seemed to be plucked from a pirate's chest.

He was just finishing his problems when a roaring sound overtook the school. The walls began to shake, the door rattled, and some of the younger children began to cry. Walter rushed to the window and was stunned by what he saw.

"It was like day had turned to night," one farmer later wrote in his journal. From out of nowhere, sheets of snow and ice pounded the school.

Fortunately the men of the small, tight-knit town of Groton mobilized quickly when the storm hit. As the teachers gathered the children in front of the school, they were relieved to discover that five enormous horse-drawn sleds were already there, ready to take everyone home. The teachers kept careful track of every child who climbed onto a sled, checking off names in their attendance books. When every child was accounted for, the sleds began to move.

SWALLOWED BY DARKNESS

Walter's sled was creeping slowly away from the school when he remembered his perfume bottle. He knew the delicate glass would never survive in such cold temperatures: The water inside would freeze, and the bottle would shatter.

Nobody saw Walter Allen as he jumped down from the sled and hurried back into the school. It took him just a few seconds to grab his bottle, stuff it into his pocket, and rush back outside.

But the sleds had vanished — swallowed by

the sudden darkness. Walter tried to run into the street, but the wind spun him and knocked him over. He stood up, took two steps, and the wind swatted him down again. Up and down, up and down.

Meanwhile, snow and ice swarmed around Walter's body like attacking bees. Snow blew up his nose, into his eyes, and down the collar of his shirt. His face became encrusted in ice, and his eyes were soon sealed shut by his frozen tears.

He managed to stand one final time, desperate now. But he was no match for this monstrous storm. Once more the wind slammed Walter down. This time he could not stand up, so he curled himself into a ball, too exhausted to move. He realized that nobody knew that he wasn't on the sleds, huddled among classmates, heading for home. It was as though he had tumbled off Earth and into space — a frozen, swirling darkness.

THE LONG WINTER

Brutal winters were always a part of life on America's northern plains. Native American tribes first settled the area 1,500 years ago, hunting buffalo across the flat, grassy plains. But most tribes migrated south for the winters, returning after the worst of the snows had passed.

Few of the white settlers who came to the plains were prepared for the hardships and loneliness of life on the prairie. Many were driven away — or

A young steer after a blizzard

killed — by the deadly winters. "There was nothing in the world but cold and dark and work . . . and winds blowing," remembers Laura Ingalls Wilder in her book *The Long Winter*. The book, part of the famous Little House series, describes the Ingalls family's terrifying experiences in the Dakota Territory during the snowy winter of 1880–81. At one point, trains carrying food and coal were stranded due to snowdrifts. The family and others in the town nearly starved.

But the storm of 1888 was different from even the most brutal prairie blizzards. It hit so suddenly — a gigantic wave of wind, ice, and snow that crashed over the prairie without warning. As Walter Allen lay freezing on the ground in Groton, thousands of other children across the Great Plains were also caught in the storm.

Some teachers had kept their children at school, gathering them together in front of wood-burning stoves, calming the young ones with stories and songs. Minnie Freeman, a seventeen-year-old teacher in Mira Valley, Nebraska, hoped to keep her sixteen students safe in their tiny schoolhouse. But within an hour, the winds had ripped a hole in the roof, and Minnie knew they would all freeze unless they found shelter. She tied the children together with a rope and led them through the storm, sometimes crawling along the ground to escape the winds. Somehow they made it to the boardinghouse where Minnie lived — cold but alive.

RESCUE MISSION

There were other lucky children that day, saved by quick-thinking teachers or, more often, small miracles. There were the Graber boys, who were lost on the prairie until they glimpsed a familiar tree, enabling them to find their bearings and get to their home. There was eleven-year-old Stephan Ulrich, who was lost, freezing, and nearly blind when he crashed into the side of a barn. Feeling his way to the entrance, he went inside and spent the night curled up next to a hog, whose warmth protected him from the cold.

When Walter Allen's father, W. C., discovered that his youngest son hadn't come home, he and four other men headed back to the school, risking their lives. At the last moment, they allowed Walter's eighteen-year-old brother, Will, to join

Workers dig out a train stuck in the snow.

them. Will had always watched over his little brother; he refused to stay behind.

The search party made it to the school, but Walter was nowhere to be found. W. C. became so distraught that his neighbors had to carry him back to the sled. Somehow in the sadness and confusion, they left without Will. And now both Allen boys were lost in the storm.

Although Will saw the sleds pull away, he remained focused on his search. He got down on his hands and knees and crawled along the frozen ground, feeling his way across every inch. He could not see or hear, and the wind made it difficult to breathe. But he kept searching until he bumped into a small heap covered with snow.

It was Walter. He was unconscious, but alive.

MORE PRECIOUS

During the hours that Will and Walter were fighting for their lives, hundreds of other children were caught in the grip of this killer storm.

Hundreds never made it. Even decades later, Will Allen could not explain how he managed to carry his unconscious brother through the blowing snow, or how he managed to find his way home. It was as though the storm's fury had entered Will's veins, giving him the strength to walk against the wind, to rise up when he fell, to hold his little brother tight in his arms.

They arrived home to the jubilation of their parents. Over the next few hours, Walter drifted in and out of consciousness as his family hovered over him. They warmed him slowly. They quieted his shivers. At first his body was so numb that he didn't feel the tiny cuts on his leg from the shards of glass sticking out of his pocket. It wasn't until later that night that Walter realized his beloved perfume bottle had broken during the storm after all.

Of course by then it didn't matter. Walter understood that something infinitely more precious had survived the blizzard, something that could never be replaced: Walter himself.

THE BLIZZARD FILES

This article on the Children's Blizzard was one of my favorites to research and write. I learned so much about life on the prairie — and other amazing facts. Turn the page to learn more about the Children's Blizzard, other snow disasters, and facts that I just had to share.

Picture millions of these in your yard. Ack!

There were two terrible blizzards in 1888!

THE CHILDREN'S BLIZZARD

"Heartbreaking. . . . This account of the 1888 blizzard reads like a thriller."
—ENTERTAINMENT WEEKLY

DAVID LASKIN

One of my favorite books ever!

Where I discovered the story of Walter

IF YOU LIVED DURING THE CHILDREN'S BLIZZARD...

A family in front of their sod house in Nebraska

Many settlers lived in one-room sod houses, which were made from bricks of hard-packed dirt and grass. Cold in the winter, hot in the summer, and filled with snakes and insects in the spring, these houses were anything but cozy.

Your walk to school could have taken over an hour!

A one-room schoolhouse

The school was often just one room where kids of all ages were taught by a single teacher.

States and Territories
of the United States
of America,
May 17, 1884, to
November 2, 1889

Your teacher might have lived with you.

Your teacher might be very young — as young as sixteen or seventeen. She (most teachers were female) would have lived with a family in town or in a boardinghouse.

Your chores would start hours before school.

Kids on the plains woke up early to milk cows, get water, make a fire, feed the animals, or do other chores before school even started. Girls helped in the kitchen. Doing laundry might take an entire day.

A LAND OF EXTREMES

Blizzards, Droughts, Tornadoes, Prairie Fires, Hailstorms ... and Grasshoppers!

There is no place on earth with more extreme weather conditions than America's northern plains.

But if that isn't bad enough, get ready for grasshoppers, also known as locusts. Swarms containing billions of the insects would sweep down from the sky and devour everything in their path. Many farms were destroyed by locusts, which often struck just before a harvest. In a matter of hours, an entire year's work would be gone.

A grasshopper, aka a locust

PRAIRIE is the French word for "grassland."

WORST BLIZZARDS IN US HISTORY

These storms set records for snow, wind, and the number of people killed.

 1 The Great Blizzard of 1888, March 11-14, 1888

AFFECTED AREAS: Connecticut, New York, New Jersey, and Massachusetts

DEATHS: 400

Believe it or not, an even more deadly blizzard struck the United States just two months after the Children's Blizzard. On March 11, 1888, a "white hurricane" struck. The worst of the storm lasted a day and a half, and buried some areas in more than five feet of snow. Winds howled. Trees fell. Houses were buried. Because this storm hit big cities and towns, it affected millions more people than the Children's Blizzard. In fact, historians call it the Great Blizzard of 1888. And it is usually ranked as the worst in US history.

1888: THE YEAR OF THE BLIZZARDS

Continued >

The Brooklyn Bridge after the storm

A Brooklyn
neighborhood

The Great Appalachian Storm, November 24–30, 1950

AFFECTED AREAS: Eastern United States
DEATHS: 353

 ## The Storm of the Century, March 11–15, 1993

AFFECTED AREAS: Canada all the way down to Central America; twenty-two states and 40 percent of the US population were affected.
DEATHS: 318

QUESTION: Should blizzards be named, like hurricanes are?

 ## The Great Lakes Storm of 1913

AFFECTED AREAS: Great Lakes region
DEATHS: 250

Snowmageddon Blizzard, February 4–6, 2010

AFFECTED AREAS: Mid-Atlantic states
DEATHS: 13

 ## Blizzard or Snowstorm?

The difference between a snowstorm and a blizzard is wind, not the amount of snow. Blizzards have strong winds that blow snow, which makes it hard to see. Otherwise it's just a regular old snowstorm.

FRANK LESLIE'S
ILLUSTRATED
·BLIZZARD·
NEWSPAPER

No. 1,695.—Vol. LXVI.]   NEW YORK—FOR THE WEEK ENDING MARCH 24, 1888.   [Price, 10 Cents.

THE GREAT STORM OF MARCH 12TH-13TH.—SCENE IN PRINTING-HOUSE SQUARE, NEW YORK CITY, SHOWING THE TERRIBLE FORCE OF THE BLIZZARD.

Frank Leslie's Illustrated Newspaper
shows the amount of snow in Printing-
House Square, New York City, during the
Great Blizzard of 1888.

MY RESEARCH JOURNEY

LAURA INGALLS WILDER

The Long Winter

ILLUSTRATED BY GARTH WILLIAMS

THE SPARK

I first read the Little House books when I was already grown up. *The Long Winter* is my favorite. It sparked my interest in the history of America's northern prairie.

FINDING THE STORY

This is the most important book on the blizzard, packed with stories and insights that come from the author's incredible research. It was in Mr. Laskin's book that I discovered the story of Walter Allen, just one of many stories of survival that the author uncovered from that day.

TRACKING DOWN THE DETAILS

I filled in many details from books about prairie life and with resources I discovered online, from the Google Earth view of the Dakota Territory (now North and South Dakota) to newspapers published in the days after the storm.

#2

THE TITANIC
DISASTER, 1912

In just a few hours, the *Titanic* would be at the bottom of the Atlantic Ocean. Some 1,500 people — men, women, and children — would be dead.

Yet at 11:00 that night, April 14, 1912, there was not the slightest hint of doom in the air. Jack Thayer, seventeen, had come outside to admire the brilliant sky before going to bed. The stars were so sparkly they reminded Jack of diamonds. The ocean was perfectly calm. All was quiet except for the steady hum of the ship's engines and the whistle of a gentle breeze.

Workers stand under the *Titanic*'s massive propellers.

"It was the kind of night," Jack would later recall, "that made one glad to be alive."

Indeed, this smart and curious boy from Philadelphia had much to feel glad about. He and his parents were returning from a two-month trip to Europe. Everywhere Jack looked, he saw signs of a fast-changing world — a world made brighter by new electric lights, made faster by motorcars and powerful steam engines, and made safer by breakthroughs in science.

The *Titanic* was a symbol of all of these changes — the biggest, most elegant, most technologically advanced ship ever built. How lucky Jack felt to be on its first voyage across the Atlantic.

Jack Thayer in 1912, age 17

Even the Thayers, who lived in a mansion and had traveled the world, were dazzled by the grandeur of the ship. It was the most expensive ship ever built. Eleven stories high and as long as four city blocks, it was the world's largest man-made moving object.

As three of *Titanic*'s 324 first-class passengers, the Thayers enjoyed a level of glittering luxury never before offered at sea. They had their choice of three restaurants, each offering a seemingly endless selection of fine dishes. Dinner might be eleven different courses, beginning with a velvety soup and ending with a selection of cakes and puddings and pastries made by a famous French chef.

After dinner, Jack and his parents could dance to the music of an orchestra, or pass the evening playing cards in the elegant library. There was a swimming pool — the first ever built on a ship — filled with warmed ocean water. And, of course, there were the fine sleeping cabins and spacious rooms furnished with beautiful antiques and chandeliers. The Thayers, along with the other first-class passengers, had paid more than four thousand dollars each for a ticket. It surely was a fortune — more than what most people in 1912 would pay for a house. But Jack's family could easily afford it. And it was well worth the cost for this chance to be a part of history.

Most of the passengers were not rich like the Thayers. In fact, the majority were crowded onto the lower decks, in third class. Many of these

Luxury ships like the *Titanic* included first-class amenities.

A first-class menu from the *Titanic*

The *Titanic* gymnasium with cycling racing machines

The first-class dining saloon on the *Olympic*, *Titanic*'s sister ship. *Titanic*'s dining saloon was almost identical.

passengers were poor families, crossing the ocean to start new lives in America. Cabins were cramped and dark, with bunk beds and simple wooden chests. In the third-class dining room, families dined on simple foods — porridge for breakfast, codfish cakes for dinner — at long wooden tables. The air was stuffy, and it was filled with echoes of crying babies and chattering in dozens of different languages.

Third-class passengers were not permitted on the elegant upper deck, where the Thayers mingled with their fellow first-class passengers. Most of the men were successful businessmen, like Jack's father, but there were other fascinating people on board — doctors, artists and writers, even a famous tennis player.

Jack especially enjoyed his conversations with Thomas Andrews, the architect of the *Titanic*. The Irishman could talk for hours about the wonders of the ship, and Jack never tired of listening. Andrews was modest. But he couldn't deny that the *Titanic*'s maiden voyage was a magnificent success. In three days, the ship was due to arrive in New York. Crowds of reporters and photographers would be waiting, along with hundreds of cheering spectators. Already Jack could feel the excitement.

"UNSINKABLE"

It was almost eleven-thirty when Jack went back to his cabin, which was next to his parents' suite. He called good night to his mother and father.

An advertisement for the *Titanic* shows the first-class deck.

Just as he was about to get into bed, he swayed slightly. He realized the ship had veered to the left — "as though she had been gently pushed," he would later say.

The engines stopped, and for a moment, there was a quiet that was "startling and disturbing."

Then Jack heard muffled voices and running footsteps. He threw on his overcoat and slippers, told his parents he was going to see what was happening, and rushed outside. Soon a crowd of first-class passengers, including his father, joined him. Jack wasn't worried. Actually there was a mood of adventure, especially after news spread that the ship had struck an iceberg. The men in the crowd joked and puffed on cigars as they craned their necks and squinted into the dark night. They all wanted to see the object that had dared interrupt the voyage of the great *Titanic*. Chunks of ice had fallen onto the other decks. Passengers played rowdy games of catch with balls of ice, tossing them back and forth as they laughed with delight.

"Nobody yet thought of any serious trouble," Jack would recall. "The ship was unsinkable."

That's certainly what most people believed: that the *Titanic*'s state-of-the-art safety features — sixteen watertight compartments to contain flooding — would keep the ship afloat no matter what. So it was with no sense of worry that Jack and his father roamed the ship, trying to find out when they would again be under way.

But then Jack and his father saw Mr. Andrews, the ship's designer, standing with several of the ship's officers. Andrews's grave expression sent a stab of fear through Jack's heart. If anyone understood what was really happening on the *Titanic*, it was the man who knew the ship inside and out.

And the truth was terrifying. The iceberg's jagged fingers had clawed through the steel hull. Water was gushing into the ship's lower levels.

"The *Titanic* will sink," Andrews said. "We have one hour."

That, though, was only half of the horrifying story. As Jack would soon learn, the *Titanic* had twenty lifeboats. That was more than the law required. But it was only enough for about half of the passengers and crew. Looking around the ship, he knew that many of the passengers were doomed. The *Titanic* was eight hundred miles from New York. The temperature of the ocean was 28 degrees Fahrenheit. Immersed in water that cold, a human body goes into shock almost immediately. The heart slows. The skin begins to freeze. Death comes within eighty minutes.

For those who couldn't escape by lifeboat, there was almost no hope of survival.

LOST IN THE CROWD

Jack put on a warm wool suit and a sweater. He tied on his life preserver and slipped into his overcoat, and then he rushed back up to the deck with his parents. What they found was confusion and noise — people shouting, rockets being fired into the air. Jack was with his parents and his mother's maid, Margaret Fleming. A young man named Milton Long, whom Jack had befriended at dinner earlier that night, soon joined them. The group made their way through the ship, hoping to find a lifeboat.

Suddenly they were in the middle of a crowd of panicked passengers. To Jack's horror, he and Milton were separated from his parents and Margaret. He searched desperately but could not find them. He became convinced that they had all boarded a lifeboat, leaving him behind. And there were no lifeboats left.

Jack and Milton were on their own.

Amid the noise and panic, the screams and shouts and explosions, Jack and Milton tried to bolster each other's courage as the ship continued to sink. "I sincerely pitied myself," Jack said, "but we did not give up hope."

They decided that their best chance for survival was to wait until the ship was low enough in the water that they could jump in without injuring themselves. This would be difficult. Already the water around the ship was filled with chairs and objects that had slid off the sinking ship. If Jack hit something on his way down, he could be knocked unconscious. But Jack tried not to think about that as he waited for the right time.

That moment came at about 2:15 A.M. The ship lurched forward, its bow plunging deeper into the black waters of the Atlantic. Jack and Milton shook hands and wished each other luck.

Milton went first, climbing over the railing and sliding down the side of the ship. Jack would never see him again.

Jack threw off his overcoat and, he later said, "With a push of my arms and hands, [I] jumped into the water as far out from the ship as I could. . . . Down, down I went, spinning in all directions."

He struggled to the surface, gasping from the cold, his lungs near bursting. He had been floating for only a few minutes when one of the ship's enormous funnels broke free. In a shower of sparks and black smoke, it crashed into the water just twenty feet from Jack. The suction pulled him under the water once again. This time he barely made it back up.

But as he surfaced, his hand hit something — an overturned lifeboat. Four men were balancing on its flat bottom. One of them helped Jack up. From there, they watched the *Titanic* in its final agonizing moments — the stern rising high into the sky, hundreds of people dropping into the sea, the lights finally going out.

Then, in a moment of eerie quiet, the ship disappeared into the dark water.

"A WAILING CHANT"

The silence was broken by the first frantic cries for help. People — hundreds of them — were

A photographer on the
Carpathia captures
Titanic survivors
huddled on a lifeboat.

scattered everywhere in the water, kept afloat by their life vests. The individual cries became "a continuous wailing chant" of terror and pain and desperation, Jack said.

Over the next few minutes, he and the others on the lifeboat managed to pull twenty-four men out of the water alive. The group was "packed like sardines" on the boat, their arms and legs tangled together. Freezing waves washed over them. Nobody moved for fear of slipping into the water.

Little by little, the terrible wailing faded.

Floating in the silent blackness, numb with cold and terror, Jack waited for death.

But then came a light — at 4:10 A.M., a ship called the *Carpathia* broke through the darkness. Its captain had received the *Titanic*'s distress call and rushed his ship through the icy waters. Among the first faces Jack saw when he boarded the rescue ship was his mother's. Margaret was also aboard.

The joy of their reunion was overwhelming — but so was the shock when Jack's mother asked a simple question.

"Where is your father?"

As it turned out, Mr. Thayer had not boarded a lifeboat.

"Of course, I should have known that he would never have left without me," Jack later said.

The *Carpathia*, carrying the *Titanic*'s 705 grief-stricken survivors, docked in New York City on April 18, and was greeted by a crowd of thirty

A newsboy, Ned Parfett, holds a paper announcing the sinking of the Titanic.

thousand people. For months after, the *Titanic* was front-page news. People around the world demanded answers. How could the mighty *Titanic* be lost? Who was to blame? There was no doubt that *Titanic*'s crew knew that there were icebergs looming in the North Atlantic. Indeed, they had received several urgent warnings from ships traveling the same route. And yet the ship had been traveling at high speeds. Many wondered if the ship's captain, Edward Smith, had felt pressure to make the voyage as speedy as possible, to showcase *Titanic*'s state-of-the-art engines. But Captain Smith went down with his ship, as did Mr. Andrews and other senior members of the crew.

And so in the end, many directed their fury toward a man named Bruce Ismay. He was the president of the company that owned the *Titanic*, the White Star Line. Ismay had been on the ship's doomed voyage. Unlike *Titanic*'s captain and Mr. Andrews, Mr. Ismay had escaped on a lifeboat.

Ismay was accused of ordering Captain Smith to ignore the iceberg risks. Some reports even suggested that he had pushed aside women and children to take a precious spot on a lifeboat. There was no proof of any of this.

Edward J. Smith, captain of the *Titanic*

Ismay denied that he'd pressured Captain Smith to ignore the iceberg warnings. And those who knew Captain Smith doubted that the respected seaman would knowingly endanger his ship and passengers. Ismay insisted that the lifeboat he'd boarded had been half-empty, and witnesses supported this. In fact, many saw Ismay helping women and children onto the boats, and assisting the crew in lowering the boats into the sea. The British government cleared Ismay of any wrong-doing. But his reputation never recovered, and he was forever branded a coward.

After docking in New York, Jack and his mother returned to Philadelphia. He wrote a long letter to the parents of Milton Long, describing their friendship and their last moments together. Jack went on to marry, have two sons, and attain a powerful position at the University of Pennsylvania. Years later he wrote his own account of the sinking of the *Titanic*, dedicated to his father's memory. In it he described his last glimpse of the

The *New York Times* describes the *Titanic* disaster and provides a partial list of those saved.

ship, breaking in two as it sank. Most experts disputed this. But many decades later, when the wreckage of the *Titanic* was finally located, Jack's account was proven correct.

Today, more than one hundred years after the ship's sinking, stories of its survivors still fascinate and inspire. In this way the mighty ship sails on.

Said to be Jack Thayer's description of the *Titanic's* sinking, sketched by Thayer and filled in later by L. P. Skidmore

11:45 P.M. Strikes starboard bow
12:05 A.M. Settles by head
12:45 A.M. Boats ordered out
1:40 A.M. Settles to forward stack
             Breaks between stacks

1:50 A.M. Forward end floats, then sinks
2:00 A.M. Stern section pivots amidships and
  swings over spot where forward section sank
Last position in which *Titanic* stayed, five minutes
  before the final plunge
L. P. Skidmore, S.S. *Carpathia*, April 15, 1912

THE TITANIC FILES

There are more books written about the *Titanic* than any other disaster in history, and I read dozens of them while researching my book, *I Survived the Sinking of the* Titanic, *1912.* That's when I first discovered the story of Jack Thayer — plus many other amazing facts and details about the ship and its tragic voyage. Turn the page to find out more.

Saved from the wreckage!

The Titanic used 800 tons a day of this!

SOME SURPRISING TITANIC FACTS

COST The ship **cost** $7.5 million to build. That equals $185 million in today's dollars, about the same price as building one Boeing 767 jet.

SPEED *Titanic*'s top **speed** was 23 knots, which is 26 miles per hour. Today's cruise ships can move much faster, but most actually maintain speeds that are slower than the *Titanic*'s, about 22 knots. The reason? Moving faster burns more fuel, which costs more money.

POWER *Titanic* was **steam powered**. Steam was created by burning massive amounts of coal. It took two hundred men — stokers, firemen, and trimmers — to tend to the ship's 162 coal furnaces. The ship burned eight hundred tons of coal each day.

Coal

PASSENGERS There were 1,317 **passengers** on the ship, only about half as many as there was room for. A strike of coal workers in England had caused many people to postpone their travel plans. The strike had ended only a few days before *Titanic* sailed.

TICKET PRICE

The **most expensive ticket** was about $4,500, equivalent to about $103,000 in today's dollars. The cheapest tickets cost about $40, about $172 today — the same as it might cost to fly today from New York to Miami.

A first-class ticket from the Titanic

The ship's cargo included huge amounts of **food** for the passengers and crew — 40 tons of potatoes, 40,000 eggs, 6,000 apples, and 86,000 pounds of meat.

Eight hundred eighty-five people made up *Titanic*'s **crew**. Sixty-six worked on the decks, 325 were in the engine room, and the rest were maids, stewards, cooks, waiters, and others who tended to the passengers.

LAST LETTER

The **last letter** written on *Titanic* recently sold for more than $200,000. It was written by survivors Esther Hart and her seven-year-old daughter Eva eight hours before the ship hit the iceberg. Mrs. Hart wrote that they were enjoying "a wonderful journey."

FINDING THE *TITANIC*

The *Titanic* was lost in the North Atlantic, eight hundred miles from land. For decades people searched for the wreckage. Finally, on September 2, 1985, the *Titanic* was found by Dr. Robert Ballard.

Dr. Robert Ballard

THE *ALVIN*, a research submarine that was used in the discovery of the *Titanic* wreckage

TREASURE TROVE OR GRAVEYARD?

Dr. Ballard and others believe that the *Titanic* should not have been touched — that it is a graveyard. Others disagree. They say that bacteria and salt water will slowly eat away at what remains and that artifacts should be collected and studied. There have been eight expeditions to the *Titanic* to collect artifacts. RMS TITANIC Inc (RMTI) has recovered more than 5,500 artifacts, including some on the next pages.

The bow of the *Titanic*, on the ocean floor

Continued >

TITANIC'S PRICELESS TREASURES

Some of the thousands of dishes salvaged from the wreck were not even chipped.

A pair of binoculars

A bronze ship's bell

In 1912, glasses were called *spectacles*.

Few people wore wristwatches. Men carried pocket watches, like this one.

Lockets were extremely fashionable. Somehow, the photograph inside was not destroyed.

YES OR NO?
Should *Titanic*'s artifacts be salvaged, or left alone?

#3

THE GREAT
BOSTON MOLASSES
FLOOD, 1919

It was a sunny January day in 1919, and eight-year-old Anthony di Stasio hurried along a crowded sidewalk in Boston's North End. As usual, the streets were packed with honking motorcars and clattering horse-drawn wagons. After weeks of freezing cold, the day was warm and bright. Anthony's tattered wool coat flapped open as he rushed toward the tiny apartment where he lived with his parents and four sisters.

Like most of the people who lived in this poor Boston neighborhood, Anthony's family had come from southern Italy, eager to start a new and happier life in America. What they found instead was hardship. Jobs were scarce. Anthony's father worked long, bone-crushing hours on Boston's waterfront. Anthony's mother struggled to make their dingy apartment into a decent home — to chase away the cockroaches, to cover up the stink of garbage and horse manure that wafted up from the streets. Life had always been tough for the people of the North End. But the past two years had been especially challenging for them — and most Americans.

World War I had raged in Europe since 1914. More than four million American soldiers had joined the fight to defeat Germany and its allies. For four years the fighting had dragged on. New weapons, like the machine gun, tanks, and poisonous gas, made the battles more horrific than any before. At the war's height, tens of thousands of soldiers were dying every week. By the time the war finally ended, nearly nine million soldiers had lost their lives.

In the war's final months, another horror hit

the world: the influenza epidemic of 1918. The flu first appeared in Europe. It spread quickly through the dirty hospitals packed with wounded soldiers. Within the year it had circled the globe, killing fifty million people, including more than 650,000 Americans.

But finally, after years of terror and death, the war and the flu epidemic were over. Anthony might have even sensed a mood of hopefulness on that pleasing January day. The residents of Boston's North End had every reason to believe that better times were just ahead.

The molasses tank loomed up over Boston's North End.

They were wrong.

A shocking disaster was about to strike Anthony's neighborhood. In fact, a deadly threat had been looming over the North End for years. It was not a German bomb or a killer disease.

It was a giant steel tank filled with molasses.

FROM PIES TO BOMBS

Molasses is a thick brown syrup that was once the most popular sweetener in America. Like white sugar, molasses comes from the sugarcane plant, which grows in the Caribbean and other hot and humid regions. Until the late 1800s, white sugar was so expensive that only rich people could afford it. Molasses was cheap. So despite its bitter taste, it was molasses that sweetened colonial America's tasty treats, like pumpkin pie, gingersnaps, and Indian pudding.

By the 1900s, sugar prices had dropped, and most Americans no longer needed to sweeten their foods with cheap molasses. The sticky brown syrup was

being put to a new and
perhaps surprising use: as
an ingredient in bombs.
Heated up in a process
known as distillation,
molasses can be turned into a liquid called
industrial alcohol. In this form molasses became a
key ingredient in the explosives used in the war
against Germany.

All during World War I, ships loaded with
millions of gallons of molasses arrived at Boston's
ports. Trains would transport the gooey cargo to
distilleries, where the molasses was turned into
industrial alcohol. From there it went to factories,
where the alcohol was used to make bombs,
mines, grenades, and other weapons.

In 1914, the leaders of one molasses company,
United States Industrial Alcohol (USIA), decided
to build an enormous molasses storage tank near
Boston Harbor. The tank was constructed very
quickly, and it was massive — bigger than any

tank ever built in Boston. The company now had a place to store molasses between its arrival by ship and its journey by train. When full, the tank could hold 2.7 million gallons of molasses. As if the North End wasn't already grim enough, now a three-story steel tank towered over the neighborhood, blotting out the sun and blocking the view of the harbor.

But it wasn't only the tank's ugliness that upset the residents of the North End.

Just hours after it was first filled with molasses, brown syrup had started leaking from the seams of the tank, oozing like blood from a wounded body. When the tank was filled, it rumbled and groaned, as though the steel walls were crying out in pain. USIA's own workers reported the leaks and shared their fears that the tank was not safe. Their bosses refused to try to fix the leaks. Instead, they hired painters to coat the tank with brown paint. This way it was harder to see the brown molasses dripping down the sides.

Many people living near the tank worried it was unsafe. But what could they do about it? USIA was a big company, and the people in the North End were poor and powerless. Many did not speak English. Even a person bold enough to complain about the dangerous conditions would have had a hard time finding anyone willing to listen and help.

And so the years passed. The tank leaked so badly that neighborhood children would gather there when they wanted a sweet treat. They'd bring sticks to use as spoons and scoop up molasses from the puddles that surrounded the tank. The groaning of the steel grew louder and louder — until the moment on that January day in 1919, when Anthony di Stasio was heading home.

VIOLENT SWIRL

The first sign of disaster was a strange sound:

Rat, tat, tat, tat. Rat, tat, tat, tat. Rat, tat, tat, tat.

Many believed it was machine-gun fire and dove for cover. In fact, it was the sound of the thousands of steel rivets that held the molasses tank together popping out of place. After years of strain, the tank was breaking apart.

People froze in their tracks. Horses reared up in panic. And then came a thundering explosion.

Kaboom!

"Run!" a man screamed. "It's the tank!"

Anthony looked up just as the molasses tank seemed to crack apart like a massive egg, unleashing

Some of the wreckage after the molasses flood, with part of the collapsed tank in the background

its 2.7 million gallons of thick, sticky molasses. The molasses formed a gigantic brown wave — 25 feet high and 160 feet wide. It moved at a staggering 35 miles per hour, faster even than the modern cars that sped along the streets. The sticky syrup was far heavier and more destructive than a wave of ocean water. And unlike a wave unleashed from the sea, the molasses crashed out in all directions.

Within seconds, the wave crushed wooden houses and flattened a three-story fire station. It destroyed train tracks, swept away motorcars, crushed cars and wagons, and snapped electrical poles in half. Giant pieces of the tank's metal turned into missiles. The thousands of steel rivets shot through the sky like bullets. Anthony and dozens of others were caught in the raging swirl.

The wave pulled Anthony under. Molasses gushed into his mouth. He was carried for several blocks until he crashed into a metal lamppost. The blow knocked him out. A firefighter saw

Anthony pinned against the lamppost. Rushing through waist-deep molasses, the man grabbed Anthony just before he was swept away.

The firefighter held Anthony's limp body and looked at his molasses-coated face. The poor boy, the firefighter believed, had not survived.

By the time the wave lost its power, a half mile of the North End was flooded with molasses.

Firemen waded through knee-deep molasses.

Hundreds of firefighters, police officers, nurses, and sailors from docked ships rushed to the scene. They waded through the river of molasses to get to the trapped and injured. Many victims were caught under collapsed buildings and tangled in molasses-soaked debris. Rescuers worked through the night, bringing hundreds of people to a makeshift hospital set up in a nearby warehouse. In the end, 21 people were killed, and 150 were injured. Tens of millions of dollars in property was destroyed.

The clean-up lasted for months. Plain water did little to wash the thick, syrupy molasses away. Instead, firefighters used salt water to scour the hardening goo from the streets. Volunteers got on their hands and knees to try to scrub molasses from the streets and sidewalks. People in ground-floor apartments had to throw away their furniture and rugs. So much molasses had flowed into Boston Harbor that the water was stained caramel-brown for weeks.

An ambulance drives along the ruined streets.

THE TANK WAS BOMBED?

Within hours of the spill, leaders of USIA had announced that the disaster was not their fault. They concocted a story: A bomb had destroyed the tank. It was a lie, of course. But the story wasn't completely far-fetched. At the time, criminals known as anarchists were terrorizing people in Boston and other cities. These people hated the government and big companies. Just weeks before the molasses flood, an anarchist's bomb had destroyed a North End police station.

At first, USIA had no trouble blaming anarchists for the tank disaster. But as the police began their investigation, another story emerged. Experts sifting through the wreckage found no signs of bomb damage. As police spoke to residents, they heard about the years of leaks and strange noises that echoed from the tank. Slowly the truth came out: The tank had been hastily built, and USIA's own workers had repeatedly warned their bosses that the tank was a disaster waiting to happen.

It didn't take long for investigators to pin the blame on USIA. But still the company refused to take responsibility. At that point, there were no laws that made it illegal to build a shoddy tank in the middle of a crowded neighborhood. USIA, it seemed, would get away with murder.

A section of the collapsed molasses tank after the explosion

But people in Boston were outraged. And it would turn out that the poor immigrants of the North End weren't so powerless after all. Families who had lost relatives and homes hired lawyers and demanded justice. There was a trial that dragged on for years. In the end USIA was forced to pay one million dollars (equal to about seven million dollars today). For the residents of the North End, it was a big victory. And their case helped bring about new laws. Massachusetts was the first state to require people to get permits before constructing a tank or any structure. Building plans had to be approved before construction could begin. Similar laws were soon passed throughout the United States.

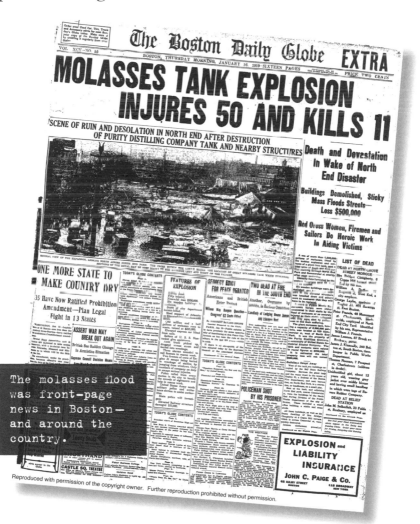

The molasses flood was front-page news in Boston— and around the country.

THE STRANGEST DISASTER

It took years for the North End to rebuild after the flood. The millions of gallons of molasses had filled basements and seeped into cracks in the street. Even now, on hot days, some claim that

Boston Molasses Flood

On January 15, 1919, a molasses tank at 529 Commercial Street exploded under pressure, killing 21 people. A 40-foot wave of molasses buckled the elevated railroad tracks, crushed buildings and inundated the neighborhood. Structural defects in the tank combined with unseasonably warm temperatures contributed to the disaster.

THE BOSTONIAN SOCIETY

A historical marker in Boston's North End is the only reminder of the flood.

the sweet scent of molasses rises up from the sidewalks of the North End, like a ghost.

But somehow this disaster has been largely forgotten. There are no museums and no monuments to those who died. The only remnant of the flood is a small metal plaque in Boston's North End. Indeed, few have ever heard of the Molasses Flood of 1919 and the incredible stories from that day — like the story of Anthony di Stasio. Anthony's limp, molasses-soaked body was taken to a large building that was being used to store the bodies of those who had died. He was covered with a sheet.

But Anthony wasn't dead, only unconscious. Hours later, he woke up to the sound of his mother's voice calling him. Anthony tried to answer. But his mouth was filled with molasses.

Suddenly he sat up. And soon he was surrounded by his family, a lucky survivor of one of the strangest disasters in American history.

THE BOSTON MOLASSES FLOOD FILES

I first heard about the Boston molasses flood from an I Survived reader, who e-mailed, "Mrs. Tarshis, you have to write about this!" I was intrigued and started researching. Like pretty much everyone who first reads about this disaster, I was shocked and amazed. How did something like this happen? Why don't we all know about it?

Read on for more about what life was like in 1919.

New technology! This brilliant invention changed the world.

Kids in 1919 played baseball just like you!

IF YOU LIVED DURING THE BOSTON MOLASSES FLOOD...

The year 1919 in America was a time of excitement and change. Over the next decade, a mood of hope brightened the country. Here's what your life might have been like if you had been living back then.

By day . . . For the first time in history, the majority of American kids were going to school. But teachers were strict! Misbehaving kids could get spanked!

Left: Students hard at work

Below: Children playing baseball in Tenement Alley, Boston

A Ford
Model T

$350:
The cost of a
Ford Model T
in 1919.

By night ... At night, you
and your family
would gather around your radio
to listen to music, news, and
radio plays.

Hop into your family's
car — a Ford Model T. This was
the world's first truly affordable
car, and soon America's streets
were crowded with them. But
be careful. Roads were terrible,
and cars, horses, and buggies
shared them. Accidents were
common, and seat belts were still
decades away.

Turn it up! Radios like this
played news, music, comedies,
and serious "radio plays."

A jazz band gets ready to play.

New music . . . Exotic sounds filled the air — a new kind of music called jazz.

New inventions . . . Few inventions in history have changed the world as quickly as Thomas Edison's lightbulb — no more candles and smelly oil lamps.

ANOTHER STRANGE AND DEADLY DISASTER:
THE GREAT MILL DISASTER, 1878

The Washburn A Mill, in Minneapolis, Minnesota, after the great explosion of 1878

The Washburn A Mill in Minneapolis, Minnesota, was the largest flour mill in the world when a spark ignited flour dust that filled the air. Eighteen people were killed in the fire and collapse of the building. The disaster made news around the world, and led to changes in the way large mills were run. The mill was quickly rebuilt and was soon back to grinding two million pounds of flour per day.

WORLD WAR I:
FOUR BLOODY YEARS

The molasses flood happened just months after the end of one of the great tragedies of the twentieth century — World War I. The war was fought mostly in Europe, with Germany leading one side and the Allied Forces of England, France, and Russia leading the other. By the time the war was finally over, in November of 1918, roughly one hundred countries felt the impact of this terrible "world war," the bloodiest the world had ever known.

At first, Americans managed to stay out of the fighting. But by April 1917 the United States could no longer stay on the sidelines. In the end, more than two million American troops headed to Europe and helped the Allied troops defeat Germany.

After the war ended, it became known as "the war to end all wars." Tragically, it was not. Twenty years later, Germany started World War II.

During World
War I, much
of the fighting
happened from
trenches, long
ditches dug
into the ground.
Trench warfare
was brutal and
miserable for
soldiers, who
lived in these
muddy pits for
weeks or months
at a time.

#4

THE JAPANESE
TSUNAMI, 2011

On the afternoon of March 11, 2011, the students and teachers of Kamaishi East Junior High School, in Kamaishi, Japan, were getting ready for after-school activities. Fourteen-year-old Aki Kawasaki was excited about basketball practice. Kana Sasaki was getting dressed for tennis. Fumiya Akasaka, captain of the boys' judo team, was heading for the gym. Shin Saito, English teacher and badminton coach, was tying his shoes. It was a typical Friday afternoon — that is, until 2:46 P.M., when a massive earthquake began to rumble twenty miles below the floor of the Pacific Ocean.

The quake, about forty miles off the northeastern shore of Japan, was a thousand times more powerful than the 2010 earthquake in Haiti. It sent shock waves hundreds of miles in every direction. In Tokyo, office buildings swayed like blades of grass. Subways stopped underground. In Kamaishi, a town on Japan's beautiful northeastern coast, buildings shook violently. Gaping holes opened in the streets.

The students and teachers of Kamaishi East rushed for cover. Computers, books, and furniture crashed to the floor around them. People screamed, but their cries couldn't be heard over the sound of the quake. That was something that people would talk about for years to come — the sound of the earthquake's roar, as if a monstrous beast had awakened deep inside the earth.

Most earthquakes last for just a few seconds, blasting out quick bursts of destruction. This quake was different. It went on and on, like an endless nightmare. It continued for nearly six minutes — the shaking, the roaring, the crashing, the shattering terror. When the earth finally stopped shaking, there was a moment of eerie quiet.

Like most schools in Japan, the Kamaishi East building had been carefully built to withstand earthquakes. Even after six minutes of violent shaking, the building stood strong. Fortunately none of the students and teachers was seriously injured.

But there was no feeling of relief for Aki, Kana, Fumiya, or any of the other students at Kamaishi East. They knew that the disaster was just beginning.

The quake under the ocean floor had triggered a tsunami, a series of massive waves. The waves were hundreds of miles wide and were racing across the ocean at jet speeds. Just a few yards high at first, the waves would grow stronger and bigger. In some places, they would reach as high as 133 feet as they approached the shore. Within

The Great Wave off Kanagawa, a nineteenth-century woodblock print by Japanese artist Hokusai

thirty minutes, the waves would hit Japan's northeastern coast with the force of the most powerful bombs.

EARTHQUAKE WARNINGS

Few places on Earth are as prone to earthquakes and tsunamis as Japan. Small quakes hit the country every single day. Most are so mild that the ground barely shakes. But over the past century alone, major earthquakes have turned modern cities to rubble. The worst was in 1923, when a major quake hit Tokyo. Fires broke out, and within days much of the city was a smoldering ruin. More than 140,000 people died. Other major quakes have caused devastating damage to the cities of Kyoto and Kobe.

Over the past few decades, Japan has done more than any other country to protect its citizens from earthquakes. Building laws are strict. Newer skyscrapers, schools, and other structures are designed to sway, rather than crumble, when the ground below shakes.

Japan also has the world's most advanced earthquake-warning system. Sensors around the country can detect the very first stages of an earthquake, the first shock waves that happen minutes before the most serious shaking begins. Alerts are sent out over cell phones. These few precious minutes of warning can mean the difference between life and death. Drivers can

TSUNAMI HAZARD ZONE

IN CASE OF EARTHQUAKE, GO TO HIGH GROUND OR INLAND

Signs like these can be found all along Japan's coasts.

pull off to the side of a highway. Subway conductors can halt their trains. Doctors and nurses can stop a delicate surgery before the shaking starts.

Japan also has a system designed to protect against tsunamis. In fact, Kamaishi was famous throughout Japan for the world's largest tsunami wall. The gigantic barrier of steel and concrete was one mile long, 297 feet deep, and rose twenty feet above the water. It cost one billion dollars and even earned a spot in the *Guinness World Records* as the biggest seawall ever built. Tsunamis had destroyed the city twice in the past 150 years — once in 1896, and again in 1933. Town leaders believed that their new wall would hold back even the most violent tsunami waves.

But not everyone was so sure.

The leaders of Kamaishi's schools had reason to be especially worried about tsunamis. Several of the city's schools were within striking distance of large waves. If a tsunami hit, students and teachers would be in grave danger. And so, even as the giant tsunami wall was being built, the school leaders were working on their own plan for keeping students safe. The idea was that they would turn Kamaishi's middle school students into tsunami experts. The more students knew, school leaders believed, the more likely they would be to survive if a tsunami struck.

So at Kamaishi East and other middle schools, tsunami education became a part of every class. In social studies, students researched the 1933 event and other tsunamis and their effects on the city. In science, they learned how tsunamis form. In language arts, they wrote essays about the 1896 tsunami. They drew hazard maps showing the likely path of the waves. They explored the area around the school, searching out the highest points. They even learned to cook soup for people in disaster shelters.

The school also held frequent tsunami drills. Students were taught to gather outside the school while teachers took attendance. They would then wait for an announcement on the loudspeaker instructing them to walk to the "refuge area," a parking lot about a ten-minute walk away.

But when the quake struck, most students immediately realized that what they had practiced in the drills would not work. They could tell that this quake was incredibly powerful, likely stronger than any recent earthquakes. They had no doubt that a tsunami was already speeding right for them. There was no time to stand in the courtyard. The electricity had been knocked out, so no announcement would be coming. It was up to them to lead the escape, a life-or-death race with the wave. There was not one minute to spare. With panicked shouts, students urged their

The
coast at
Minamisoma,
Fukushima,
on March
11, 2011

teachers to follow them as they rushed for higher ground.

"Before I realized I was running, my feet were moving," Kana would later say.

Teachers at the elementary school next door had planned to keep their young students on their building's third floor. The sight of the older students rushing away changed their minds. Soon hundreds of students and teachers were in a frantic dash for safety. Older children grabbed the younger ones and carried them on their backs.

"I thought the tsunami would come," said Aki. "I was desperately trying to escape."

They reached the parking-lot refuge area but decided that it was not high enough. Again, older students helped the younger ones, grabbing their hands, pushing them along.

They continued on, climbing higher into the hills. They finally came to rest in a parking lot on a hill. Terrified and out of breath, they had a clear view of the horrific scene unfolding in their city just below.

A BLACK RAGING RIVER

The ocean had begun its attack. Just thirty minutes after the earthquake, a black wave hit. The tsunami wall crumbled like a sand castle. Many people had climbed up onto the wall, believing they'd be safe. All were swept away. Water rushed into the streets, rising so quickly that cars, trucks, homes, and people were swallowed in seconds.

While the tsunami floods Iwaki City, fires start to burn.

The water — now a black raging river filled with debris, boats, and wrecked homes — rushed deeper into the city and up into the hills. The students watched in shock as their school was engulfed. At the elementary school, a car, lifted by the waters, crashed into the building's third floor, exactly where the teachers had planned to wait with the children after the quake. If they had stayed, they would have likely been killed.

Similar scenes were unfolding up and down Japan's coast. In a matter of minutes, hundreds of small cities, bustling towns, quaint fishing villages, and quiet farming communities were disappearing under the water. The seawater traveled farther inland than anyone imaged it could. Miles from the ocean, towns were overwhelmed.

And then, like a monster returning to its lair, the water was sucked back into the Pacific Ocean. Thousands of people who had survived the quake and the waves were swept out to sea.

Up and down Japan's coast were unreal sights, like this boat perched on a rooftop in the town of Otsuchi.

In the hours after the quake and the tsunami, Aki, Kana, and Fumiya stood amid a group of hundreds of stunned students and teachers. They eventually made their way to one of the city's surviving school buildings, where they found no food, water, or lights. They spent the night there, shivering in the cold, terrified for their families.

They went to another school the next day, and the full picture of the disaster started to become clear. They learned that much of Kamaishi was gone, that hundreds of people had died and many

Kamaishi East Junior High School students Kana
Sasaki (left), Fumiya Akasaka (center), and
Aki Kawasaki

more were missing. Most of the students' homes were lost. Fourteen students lost one or both parents. Aki, Kana, and Fumiya were among the lucky: Their families were safe.

FINDING HOPE

The disaster that hit Japan on March 11, 2011, is now known as the Great Tohoku Earthquake. The earthquake was the strongest to ever strike Japan and the fourth most powerful in all of recorded history. But it was the tsunami that caused most of the death and destruction.

Approximately eighteen thousand people were killed. One hundred thousand buildings were destroyed. In some areas of the coast, the water rose to a staggering 133 feet. Hundreds of communities were destroyed — bustling cities, beautiful villages, vibrant towns, centuries-old neighborhoods. For miles in every direction, there was nothing left but toxic mud littered with the wreckage of homes and businesses. Tanker ships had been dragged miles from the sea. Smashed cars teetered on buildings.

Japanese soldiers stand in the street to look at a ship that blocks the road.

The streets of Kesennuma City are flooded
after the tsunami.

And there was another disaster unfolding, in a
town called Fukushima. Tsunami waves had
badly damaged two nuclear power plants. Toxic
radiation was leaking into the air, endangering
hundreds of thousands of people. As far away as

Tokyo, 150 miles away, many people braced for a full-blown nuclear meltdown. This kind of nuclear disaster had happened only once before in history, in Chernobyl, a town located in what is now the country of Ukraine. Today, hundreds of square miles around the ruined Chernobyl power plant are so poisoned by radiation that no humans live there. For weeks after the quake and tsunami, many feared that the same could happen in Japan. It is hard to imagine the horror and fear that gripped the country.

To commemorate the first anniversary of the disaster, students stood vigil along the beaches throughout Japan.

But amid the hopelessness, many found inspiration in the story of the students of Kamaishi East. Not one student or teacher died in the disaster. The story of the students quickly spread around the country. Most agree it was the years of preparation and the quick-thinking students that made the difference.

"I wouldn't be here today if it wasn't for them," Mr. Sato said. "And it's the students who have given us hope and the strength to move on."

THE TSUNAMI FILES

The events of March 11, 2011, are now known as the Great Tohoku Earthquake and Tsunami. It was actually three terrible disasters bundled together — the powerful quake, the hundreds-miles-wide tsunami, and the ongoing nuclear disaster. Years later, most of the ruined areas have been cleaned up and rebuilt. But many challenges remain. Read on to learn more.

The tsunami leveled dozens of towns and villages along hundreds of miles of the coast. But today, most have been rebuilt, like the town of Miyako pictured here.

FACTS ABOUT THE GREAT TOHOKU EARTHQUAKE AND TSUNAMI

 The Quake measured 9.0 on the Richter scale, making it the strongest earthquake ever to hit Japan since record keeping began.

 The Wave topped 133 feet in some areas, taller than a nine-story building. It traveled as far as six miles inland.

The Death Toll was approximately eighteen thousand people. Most people died in the tsunami, not the earthquake.

 The Force of the earthquake shifted Earth on its axis.

 The Wreckage totaled twenty-five million tons.

TSUNAMI is a Japanese word meaning "harbor wave."

 The Cost of rebuilding the affected areas is estimated to top three hundred billion dollars.

JAPAN'S NUCLEAR DISASTER

Before

Above, Fukushima Daiichi power plant, before
the earthquake and tsunami, and below, the plant
after the disaster

After

Even years after the earthquake and tsunami, the nuclear disaster continues in and around the Fukushima Daiichi power plant. The power plant was damaged so badly that dangerous radioactive particles were released into the air. Even small amounts of these particles are dangerous for people and animals. Large amounts are deadly. People living within 12.5 miles of the plant had to flee their towns.

Radioactive particles cannot simply be cleaned up. They remain dangerous for decades — or longer. Dozens of towns all around the plant are ghost towns. Homes and shops are abandoned. Streets are empty.

Radioactive water continues to pour out of the plant. Forty-three hundred workers, wearing protective gear, are working to clean up the plant. Experts predict it will take at least thirty years. And even then, nobody can say if anyone will be willing to live in this poisoned land.

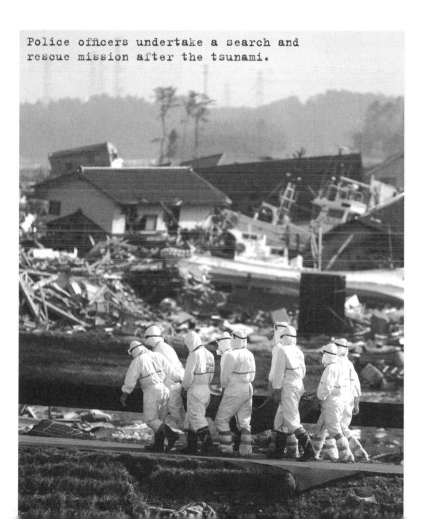

Police officers undertake a search and rescue mission after the tsunami.

EVEN SCARIER: MEGATSUNAMI

The wave that hit Kamaishi was more than a hundred feet high. Imagine if it had been one *mile* high. Sounds like science fiction. But these giant waves, known as megatsunamis, are part of Earth's natural history. These giant waves aren't triggered by earthquakes, like the Tohoku tsunami. Rather, they are caused by major volcanic eruptions, landslides, or meteorites splashing down into the ocean.

Scientists have evidence that several of these megatsunamis struck in prehistoric times. The most incredible is believed to have happened sixty-six million years ago, on the Yucatán Peninsula in Mexico. An asteroid smashed into the ocean, unleashing a towering tsunami that traveled for hundreds of miles.

#5

THE HENRYVILLE
TORNADO, 2012

Every week, I receive dozens of letters and e-mails from readers of I Survived books, but never had I gotten an e-mail like the one that appeared in my in-box on April 29, 2012.

It was from three fifth-grade girls named Shelby, Dayna, and Lyric. They were writing to tell me about a massive tornado that had struck their small town of Henryville, Indiana.

"We have so many stories to tell you about that crazy day when the tornado destroyed our school and our town," they wrote. "We want you to write our story, and we want to help you."

Four days later, I flew to Louisville, Kentucky,

and then drove twenty miles north into the beautiful green hills of southern Indiana. I met Shelby, Lyric, and Dayna, along with dozens of other students and teachers who survived the tornado. What follows is their inspiring story. I am honored to be a small part of it.

AN ORDINARY DAY

The morning of March 2, 2012, was a busy one for the fifth-grade students in Mrs. Goodknight's class at Henryville Elementary School. There was morning meeting, with poems to read, jokes to share, and tests to prepare for. Students sang "You're a Grand Old Flag" using sign language, then talked about Dr. Seuss, whose birthday was being celebrated throughout the school.

"It was just an ordinary day," said student Lyric Darling, who was twelve at the time.

Except something extraordinary was happening in the skies to the west of Henryville. Two masses of air — one warm, one cold — had collided.

Normally the meeting of two extreme weather fronts will cause a thunderstorm. But in rare cases, thunderstorms explode into larger and more savage storms known as supercells. These immense storms can move more quickly than a speeding car. With columns of swirling clouds that rise into the atmosphere more than sixty thousand feet — twice as high as Mount Everest — supercells can unleash flooding rains, destructive winds, and softball-size hailstones. Supercells can also produce the most intensely powerful force in nature: a tornado.

At noon, as Mrs. Goodknight's students were eating lunch, a line of supercells was racing toward Henryville. By recess, while students played basketball and practiced cartwheels under a sunny sky, a huge tornado was forming fifty miles away. It would soon close in on Henryville, a friendly town of two thousand people, with horse farms, businesses, and homes set amid rolling green hills.

By the end of the school day, much of Henryville would be shattered. And the lives of the seven hundred students of Henryville Elementary would be changed forever.

WHIRLWINDS AND TWISTERS

Tornadoes can — and do — strike anywhere on earth except Antarctica. But 80 percent of the world's tornadoes happen in the United States, many on the plains of the Midwest between Texas and North Dakota. This region, nicknamed Tornado Alley, provides a perfect environment for the supercells that give birth to tornadoes. Cold, dry air blasts east from the Rocky Mountains and collides with moist, warm air traveling north from the Gulf of Mexico. The fierce storms of the plains have been terrorizing humans for centuries. Native Americans told stories of whirlwinds created by the Thunderbird, a powerful god who created swirling winds by flapping his gigantic wings. American pioneers wrote horrific accounts of twisters that killed people, destroyed homes, and stripped feathers from chickens. Many of these settlers fled the region after losing their homes and barns to violent storms.

Henryville is hundreds of miles from Tornado Alley. But powerful storms often sweep through this region. Henryville students practice tornado drills every year. Just a few weeks before March 2, the threat of a tornado had forced students to evacuate their classrooms and head to refuge

A tornado on the American plains

areas. As they had practiced in their tornado drills, Mrs. Goodknight's students sat in an interior hallway near the first-grade classrooms — thought to be a safe spot — until the danger had passed.

On March 2, the National Weather Service had warned that severe storms were heading for the Henryville region. "I heard on the news that there would be high winds," said Shelby Fluhr, who was eleven at the time.

Dayna Wilson, also eleven in 2012, had heard the warning, too, before she went to school.

But Dayna, like most students, forgot about the weather as she enjoyed her busy day. "There are always warnings, but nothing bad ever happens."

DEVASTATING HIT

Around 2:25 that afternoon, less than a half hour before school was supposed to let out at Henryville Elementary, a massive tornado touched down in the town of Fredericksburg, forty miles away.

As word spread, panicked parents rushed to the school. Many people assumed that the school's principal, Dr. Glenn Riggs, would keep the students at school and have them hunker down with their teachers in the interior hallways and other refuge areas. Instead, Dr. Riggs decided that the children would be safer at home. He announced that all students were being dismissed immediately. Teachers hurried to get students onto buses or into waiting cars.

By two forty-five the skies were darkening. The air felt strange, "both hot and cold," Dayna remembered. Bus drivers raced through their routes.

"I was crying," said Lyric. "All around me, kids were crying."

As students arrived home, families rushed for shelter, grabbing pets and blankets and flashlights and other supplies. Shelby went into the storm shelter under the porch at her mother's house, cramming into the small, hot room with ten other people. Dayna's mother wasn't home, so she got off the bus with a friend, whose mother hurried them into the basement of a nearby church. Lyric and her mother went to a firehouse.

Meanwhile, the tornado was ripping a path of destruction toward Henryville. It devoured a forest, turning trees into splinters. It demolished a sturdy factory, sweeping it off its foundation and sucking much of the building into the sky. It smashed houses, snapped telephone poles, and pulled chunks of asphalt off the highway.

Two buses returned to the school with students whose parents had not been home. Staff members brought them to the office, where they all took cover under desks. Teachers followed the track of the tornado using their cell phones. But suddenly the power went out. The phones died.

"It got very dark," recalled Sally Riggs, the school's media specialist and wife of Dr. Riggs. "We were all very quiet."

And then the tornado slammed into the

The Henryville tornadoes destroyed Henryville Elementary School and many other structures in town.

school — a grinding funnel cloud a half mile wide, filled with wood and trees and glass, swirling furiously at 170 miles per hour. All around were the sounds of shattering windows, crashing walls, and objects slamming into the school. Teachers held tight to students.

"The building sounded like it was coming down around us," said Mrs. Riggs. "I didn't know if we could survive."

POUNDING FROM THE SKY

The tornado was over the school for less than one minute. In that time, it almost completely destroyed the school. The second floor collapsed. Hallways crumbled and were filled with shards of glass, splintered wood, and tiles. But miraculously none of the students or teachers was injured. Dr. Riggs led the group out of the office into a scene of devastation. An overwhelming smell of gas signaled the danger of an explosion. But before the group could leave the building, sirens began to blare and there was a new noise: "like bowling balls were being thrown at us," Mrs. Riggs said.

A second tornado was upon them. It wasn't nearly as strong as the first. But it was packed with enormous hailstones, which were now falling like cannonballs shot from the sky. They crashed through windows, windshields, and walls. When this latest attack from the sky finally ended, the dazed group made its way out of the building.

Hailstones the size of baseballs fell during the storm.

They found safety in the nearby community center.

All around town, people emerged from cellars and closets and bathrooms into a world of ruin — land swept clean of buildings and trees, homes flattened, cars smashed. The roof of the high school had been torn off, the school destroyed. A school bus had been picked up and thrown through the school's front windows.

Over the next few hours, parents arrived, overjoyed to find their children. The community braced itself for tragic news. Word came that one man had died. Many lost their homes and

Vehicles were thrown into buildings all across town.

Firefighters walk through Henryville Middle School after the tornadoes.

businesses. But by the next day, it was clear: All of Henryville's children were safe.

It was almost two months after the tornado when Dayna, Lyric, and Shelby invited me to

Jacob, Austin, Eli, and Wyatt

Emma, Erin, Sydney, and Olivia

Principal Glenn Riggs

Morgan, Jack, Collin (front), Emily, and Timmy

Henryville. I went to their temporary school, housed in a cheerful and roomy church building south of Henryville.

I met Mrs. Goodknight and Dr. and Mrs. Riggs, and I spoke to dozens of students about their experiences on March 2, 2012.

There were so many sad and frightening stories. Some students saw the tornado. Many were separated from their parents. Some students in Mrs. Goodknight's class lost their homes. A few children cried after they'd told their stories. But there were also some laughs, like when Erin told how she had found her guinea pig, alive and well, in the wreckage of her home, or when Lyric described the hailstone that's still in her freezer. Many told how the community came together to help and support one another. "You learn what's important," Mrs. Goodknight said.

Malachy, Blaine, Aden, and Joshua

Jeremiah, Isaiah (front), Noah, MaKaila, and Haylee

Les, Mrs. Riggs, Trenton, and Shelby

MaKaila, Mrs. Goodknight, Joshua, and Dillon

Each of the seven hundred children of Henryville Elementary has his or her story, and each is unique and unforgettable.

But every one of their stories ends the same way: with the incredible fact that they all survived.

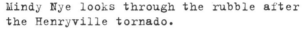
Mindy Nye looks through the rubble after the Henryville tornado.

THE TORNADO FILES

Two years after the tornado, I spoke to Mrs. Riggs, Shelby, and Lyric (Dayna had moved away). They called me from the beautiful library of their rebuilt school. What did living through the Henryville tornado teach them?

"We're blessed," Mrs. Riggs said. "People from all over the world helped us."

Shelby, Collin, Lyric, and Mrs. Riggs, April, 2014

THE 5 DEADLIEST TORNADOES IN US HISTORY

Over the centuries, twisters have left a tragic path of destruction.

 The Tri-State Tornado, March 18, 1925

AFFECTED AREAS: A single tornado left a 215-mile-long path of destruction through Missouri, Illinois, and Indiana. The tornado moved at speeds of more than 60 miles per hour, as fast as a modern car on the highway. In four hours, many communities were flattened.
DEATHS: 695

WINDS can reach up to 300 miles per hour.

 Natchez, Mississippi, May 6, 1840

AFFECTED AREAS: The massive tornado, one mile wide, ripped along the Mississippi River, destroying boats and towns along the shore.
DEATHS: 317

Tupelo, Mississippi, April 5, 1936

AFFECTED AREAS: Many city neighborhoods were destroyed. The final death count was actually far higher than the "official" one, due to the fact that in the South in 1936, officials often did not include African Americans in official counts.
DEATHS (OFFICIAL): 216

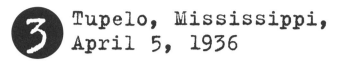 Gainesville, Georgia, April 6, 1936

AFFECTED AREAS: Just one day after the Tupelo tornado, two tornadoes merged into one massive twister, flattening homes, stores, and a large copper factory.
DEATHS: 181

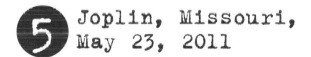 Joplin, Missouri, May 23, 2011

AFFECTED AREAS: More than one thousand homes and other buildings were destroyed by a mile-wide tornado, with winds whirling at 200 miles per hour. Entire neighborhoods were swept away.
DEATHS: 158

FOUNDING FATHER OF TORNADOES

Ben Franklin

Statesman and scientist Ben Franklin became obsessed
with tornadoes, which in the 1700s were called whirlwinds.
He studied them closely and became known as an expert.

TORNADO FACTS

An average of 1,200 tornadoes strike the United States every year.

Most tornadoes are small and last only a few minutes.

The most powerful tornadoes can reach wind speeds of 300 mph.

Tornadoes can move at speeds of 70 mph.

Most US tornadoes happen in the spring, but tornadoes can strike at any time of year.

Tornadoes that happen over water are known as water spouts.

The word TORNADO comes from two Spanish words: *tornar*, which means "to turn" and *tronada*, which means "thunderstorm."

The first record of a US tornado was written in 1680, in Cambridge, Massachusetts Bay Colony.

The largest tornado ever recorded was 2.6 miles wide, and struck on May 31, 2013, in El Reno, Oklahoma.

The brownish color of a tornado comes from the dirt and debris inside.

Sources: *Weather.com*, *US Geological Survey*, Science World *magazine*

This Doppler on Wheels radar truck is used to research tornadoes.

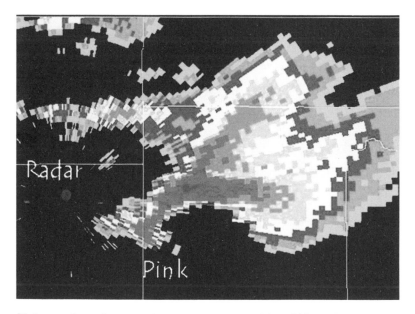

This radar image shows a supercell with a hook echo, a pattern that suggests a tornado might form.

SURVIVING A TORNADO

What should you do if a tornado is on the way?

BE AWARE Tornadoes can strike anywhere, so any time there is a serious thunderstorm, watch the TV or monitor weather websites for warnings.

DON'T TRY TO RUN Tornadoes move at highway speeds. It is not possible to outrun them.

TAKE SHELTER Underground basements are the safest place to take shelter. If one is not available, find a lower-floor closet or bathroom. Stay away from windows and top-floor rooms. Do not go outside.

STAY SAFE Danger, like downed electrical wires and gas leaks, can linger after the tornado has passed. Be careful of damaged buildings.

Source: American Red Cross

ACKNOWLEDGMENTS

I want to thank my extended *Storyworks* family —
editors, writers, designers, teacher gurus, and many
others. I am deeply grateful for these many years
of creative delights, friendship, and work that
have brought great meaning to my life. Many
dozens of people have helped make *Storyworks*
the incredible magazine it is today. Extra special
thanks to Albert Amigo, Judith Christ-Lafond,
Jennifer Dignan, Deb Dinger, Linda Eger, Allison
Friedman, David Goddy, Margaret Howlett,
Rebecca Leon, Spencer Kayden, Kristin Lewis,
Lauren Magaziner, Danielle Mirsky, Justin
O'Neill, Hugh Roome, Mary Rose, Barry Rust,
Lois Safrani, Paul Scher, Kaaren Sorensen, and
Leslie Tevlin.

MY SOURCES

Writing even a short nonfiction article requires countless hours of research. For each of the stories in this book, I relied on many sources, including books, newspaper and magazine articles, blogs, videos, maps, diaries, interviews, and face-to-face meetings.

Below are my main sources for each of the articles, including some books that you can explore.

THE CHILDREN'S BLIZZARD, 1888

The Children's Blizzard, by David Laskin, New York: HarperCollins, 2004

The Long Winter, by Laura Ingalls Wilder, New York: Harper & Bros., 1940. Paperback reprint, New York: HarperCollins, 2008

Dakota, A Spiritual Geography, by Kathleen Norris, New York: Ticknor & Fields, 1993

Great Plains, by Ian Frazier, New York: Farrar, Straus and Giroux, 1989

More books you might like:

Blizzard!: The Storm that Changed America, by Jim Murphy, New York: Scholastic, 2006

Dear America: My Face to the Wind: The Diary of Sarah Jane Price, a Prairie Teacher, Broken Bow, Nebraska, 1881, by Jim Murphy, New York: Scholastic, 2001

DK Eyewitness: Weather, by Brian Cosgrove, New York: DK Publishing, 1991

Worth, by A. LaFaye, New York: Simon and Schuster, 2004

A Year Without Rain, by D. Anne Love, New York: Holiday House, 2000

THE SINKING OF THE *TITANIC*, 1912

Titanic: A Survivor's Story and the Sinking of the S.S. Titanic, by Archibald Gracie IV and John B. Thayer, Chicago: Academy Chicago Publishers, 2005
   This includes Jack's own account of his experiences on the Titanic.

A Night to Remember, by Walter Lord, New York: Holt, 1955

The Story of the Titanic *as Told by Its Survivors*, Jack Winocour, editor, New York: Dover Publications, 1960

Titanic *Voices,* by Donald Hyslop, Alastair Forsyth, and Sheila Jemima, New York: St. Martin's Press, 1999

More books you might like:

Dear America: Voyage on the Great Titanic: *The Diary of Margaret Ann Brady, RMS* Titanic, *1912*, by Ellen Emerson White, New York: Scholastic, 1998

Discover More: Titanic, by Sean Callery, New York: Scholastic, 2014

Titanic *Trilogy: Unsinkable, Collision Couse, S.O.S.*, by Gordon Korman, New York: Scholastic, 2011.

Titanic: *Voices from the Disaster,* by Deborah Hopkinson, New York: Scholastic, 2012

I Survived the Sinking of the Titanic, *1912,* by Lauren Tarshis (of course!), New York: Scholastic, 2010

THE GREAT BOSTON MOLASSES FLOOD, 1919

Dark Tide: The Great Boston Molasses Flood of 1919, by Stephen Puleo, New York: Beacon Press, 2003
This is a complete history of the flood, and many of the details of the article are drawn from Mr. Puleo's detailed reporting.

"Boston's Great Molasses Flood, 1919," by Ethan Trex, *Mental Floss*, 2011

"The Science of the Great Molasses Flood," by Ferris Jabr, *Scientific American*, July 17, 2013

"Sweet, Sweet, Death: Boston's Molasses Flood of 1919,"
    by Ella Morton, Slate.com
"A Sticky Tragedy: The Boston Molasses Disaster," by
    Chuck Lyons, *History Today*, Volume 59, Issue 1, 2009

More books you might like:
DK Eyewitness: World War I, by Simon Adams, New
    York: DK Publishing, 2007
The Great Molasses Flood: Boston, 1919, by Deborah Kops,
    Boston: Charlesbridge, 2012
*My America: An American Spring: Sofia's Immigrant Diary,
    Book Three*, by Kathryn Lasky, New York: Scholastic,
    2004
A Place for Joey, by Carol Flynn Harris, Honesdale, PA:
    Boyds Mills Press, 2001
The War to End All Wars, by Russell Freedman, New
    York: Clarion Books, 2010
War Horse, by Michael Morpurgo, London, UK: Kaye
    and Ward, 1982. Paperback reprint, New York:
    Scholastic, 2010

THE JAPANESE TSUNAMI, 2011
The basis of my story came from an article by Setsuko
Kamayi of the *Japan Times*. She discovered the story of

Kamaichi East, and then provided additional reporting for my story, including an interview with Mr. Sato.

2:46: Aftershocks: Stories from the Japan Earthquake, by various authors, Amazon Digital Services, Inc., 2011

Facing the Wave: A Journey in the Wake of the Tsunami, by Gretel Ehrlich, New York: Vintage, 2013

Into the Forbidden Zone: A Trip Through Hell and High Water in Post-Earthquake Japan, by William T. Vollman, San Francisco: Byliner, 2011

Reconstructing 3/11, by various authors, Abiko, Japan: Abiko Free Press, 2012

Strong in the Rain: Surviving Japan's Earthquake, Tsunami, and Fukushima Nuclear Disaster, by Lucy Birmingham and David McNeill, Basingstoke, UK: Palgrave Macmillan, 2012

Japan Times, various articles by Setsuko Kamayi

"Aftershocks," by Evan Osnos, *The New Yorker,* March 28, 2011

"Tsunami Science," by Tim Folger, *National Geographic,* February 2012

"Tsunami Warnings, Written in Stone," by Martin Fackler, *The New York Times,* April 20, 2011

"Explaining Nuclear Energy for Kids," *The Washington Post*, March 17, 2011

More books you might like:

The Big Wave, by Pearl S. Buck, Philadelphia: Curtis Publishing, 1947. Paperback reprint, New York: HarperCollins, 1986

DK Eyewitness: Volcanoes and Earthquakes, by Susan van Rose, New York: DK Publishing, 2008

Sadako and the Thousand Paper Cranes, by Eleanor Coerr, New York: Puffin, 1977. Paperback reprint, 2004.

Tsunami Disasters, by John Hawkins, New York: Rosen Central, 2011

I Survived the Japanese Tsunami, 2011, by Lauren Tarshis, New York: Scholastic, 2013

THE HENRYVILLE TORNADO, 2012

I traveled to Henryville to speak to teachers and students of Henryville in May, 2013, and followed up with different students in writing and by phone.

F5: Devastation, Survival, and the Most Violent Tornado Outbreak of the Twentieth Century, by Mark Levine, New York: Miramax, 2007

Tornado Alley: Monster Storms of the Great Plains, by Howard B. Bluestein, New York: Oxford University Press, 2006

Storm Kings: The Untold History of America's First Tornado Hunters, by Lee Sandlin, New York: Pantheon, 2013

More books you might like:

DK Eyewitness: Hurricane and Tornado, by Jack Challoner, New York: DK Publishing, 2004

Tornado, by Betsy Byars, New York: HarperCollins, 1996

Tornado!: The Story Behind These Twisting, Turning, Spinning, and Spiraling Storms, by Judith Bloom Fradin and Dennis Brindell Fradin, Washington, D.C.: National Geographic, 2011

Tornadoes, by Seymour Simon, New York: HarperCollins, 2001

PHOTO CREDITS

ABOUT STORYWORKS

Storyworks is an award-winning classroom magazine read by more than 700,000 kids in grades three to six. Combining thrilling stories and articles across the genres plus amazing teacher support and online resources, *Storyworks* is a beloved and powerful language arts resource.

For more information go to:
www.scholastic.com/storyworks

Do you have what it takes?

I SURVIVED

THE SINKING OF THE *TITANIC*, 1912

UNSINKABLE. UNTIL ONE NIGHT...

George Calder must be the luckiest kid alive. He and his little sister, Phoebe, are sailing with their aunt on the *Titanic*, the greatest ship ever built. George can't resist exploring every inch of the incredible boat, even if it keeps getting him into trouble.

Then the impossible happens — the *Titanic* hits an iceberg and water rushes in. George is stranded, alone and afraid, on the sinking ship. He's always gotten out of trouble before . . . but how can he survive this?

THE SHARK ATTACKS OF 1916

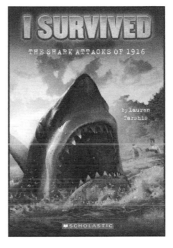

THERE'S SOMETHING IN THE WATER...

Chet Roscow is finally feeling at home in Elm Hills, New Jersey. He has a job with his uncle Jerry at the local diner, three great friends, and the perfect summertime destination: cool, refreshing Matawan Creek.

But Chet's summer is interrupted by shocking news. A great white shark has been attacking swimmers along the Jersey shore, not far from Elm Hills. Everyone in town is talking about it. So when Chet sees something in the creek, he's sure it's his imagination . . . until he comes face-to-face with a bloodthirsty shark!

I SURVIVED

HURRICANE KATRINA, 2005

HIS WHOLE WORLD IS UNDERWATER...

Barry's family tries to evacuate before Hurricane Katrina hits their home in the Lower Ninth Ward of New Orleans. But when Barry's little sister gets terribly sick, they're forced to stay home and wait out the storm.

At first, Katrina doesn't seem to be as severe a storm as forecasters predicted. But overnight the levees break, and Barry's world is literally torn apart. He's swept away by the floodwaters, away from his family. Can he survive the storm of the century — alone?

THE BOMBING OF PEARL HARBOR, 1941

A DAY NO ONE WILL EVER FORGET...

Ever since Danny's mom moved him to Hawaii, away from the dangerous streets of New York City, Danny has been planning to go back. He's not afraid of the crime or the dark alleys. And he's not afraid to stow away on the next ship out of Pearl Harbor.

But that morning, the skies fill with fighter planes. Bombs pound the harbor. Bullets rain down on the beaches. Danny is shocked — and, for the first time, he is truly afraid. He's a tough city kid. But can Danny survive the day that will live in infamy?

THE SAN FRANCISCO EARTHQUAKE, 1906

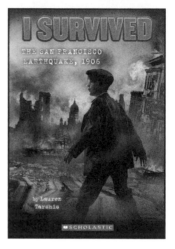

A CITY ON THE RISE — SUDDENLY FALLS...

Leo loves being a newsboy in San Francisco — he needs the money but the job also gives him the freedom to explore the amazing, hilly city as it changes and grows with the new century. Horse-drawn carriages share the streets with shiny automobiles, businesses and families move in every day from everywhere, and anything seems possible.

But early one spring morning, everything changes. Leo's world is shaken — literally — and he finds himself stranded in the middle of San Francisco as it crumbles and burns to the ground. Can Leo survive this devastating disaster?

THE ATTACKS OF SEPTEMBER 11, 2001

A DAY THAT WILL CHANGE THE NATION...

The only thing Lucas loves more than football is his dad's friend Benny, a firefighter and former football star. He taught Lucas the game and helps him practice. So when Lucas's parents decide football is too dangerous and he needs to quit, Lucas *has* to talk to his biggest fan.

On a whim, Lucas takes the train to the city instead of the bus to school. It's a bright, beautiful day in New York. But just as Lucas arrives at the firehouse, everything changes . . . and nothing will ever be the same again.

THE BATTLE OF GETTYSBURG, 1863

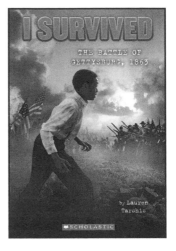

THE BLOODIEST BATTLE IN AMERICAN HISTORY IS UNDER WAY...

It's 1863, and Thomas and his little sister, Birdie, have fled the farm where they were born and raised as slaves. Following the North Star, looking for freedom, they soon cross paths with a Union soldier. Everything changes: Corporal Henry Green brings Thomas and Birdie back to his regiment, and suddenly it feels like they've found a new home. Best of all, they don't have to find their way north alone — they're marching with the army.

But then orders come through: The men are called to battle in Pennsylvania. Thomas has made it so far . . . but does he have what it takes to survive Gettysburg?

I SURVIVED

THE JAPANESE TSUNAMI, 2011

THE DISASTER FELT AROUND THE WORLD...

Visiting his dad's hometown in Japan four months after his father's death would be hard enough for Ben. But one morning the pain turns to fear: First, a massive earthquake rocks the quiet coastal village, nearly toppling his uncle's house. Then the ocean waters rise and Ben and his family are swept away—and pulled apart—by a terrible tsunami.

Now Ben is alone, stranded in a strange country a million miles from home. Can he fight hard enough to survive one of the most epic disasters of all time?

THE NAZI INVASION, 1944

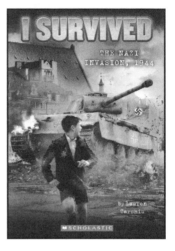

ONE OF THE DARKEST PERIODS IN HISTORY...

In a Polish ghetto, Max Rosen and his sister Zena struggle to live after their father is taken away by the Nazis. With barely enough food to survive, the siblings make a daring escape from Nazi soldiers into the nearby forest.

Max and Zena are brought to a safe camp by Jewish resistance fighters. But soon, bombs are falling all around them. Can Max and Zena survive the fallout of the Nazi invasion?

THE DESTRUCTION OF POMPEII, AD 79

THE BEAST BENEATH THE MOUNTAIN IS RESTLESS...

No one in the bustling city of Pompeii worries when the ground trembles beneath their feet. Everyone knows that the beast under the mountain Vesuvius, high above the city, wakes up angry sometimes — and always goes back to sleep.

But Marcus is afraid. He knows something is terribly wrong — and his father, who trusts science more than mythical beasts, agrees. When Vesuvius explodes into a cloud of fiery ash and rocks fall from the sky like rain, will they have time to escape — and survive the complete destruction of Pompeii?

How are YOUR survival skills? Take the quiz and learn more about real-life disasters at
SCHOLASTIC.COM/ISURVIVED

ABOUT THE AUTHOR

Lauren Tarshis is the editor of Scholastic's *Storyworks* magazine and group editorial director for language arts for Scholastic classroom magazines, in addition to being the author of the *New York Times* and *USA Today* bestselling I Survived series and the critically acclaimed novels *Emma-Jean Lazarus Fell Out of a Tree* and *Emma-Jean Lazarus Fell in Love*. She lives in Westport, Connecticut, and can be found online at LaurenTarshis.com.